SPECIAL DAYS
HARMONY DAY
CAROLINE THOMAS
REDBACK
publishing

First published 2025 by
Redback Publishing
Suite 6, 13a Narabang Way,
Belrose NSW 2085
Australia

www.redbackpublishing.com
orders@redbackpublishing.com

ISBN 978-1-761401-01-5

Author: Caroline Thomas
Editing: Simone Saba
Design: Redback Publishing

Original illustrations © Redback Publishing 2025
Originated by Redback Publishing

Acknowledgements
Abbreviations: l—left, r—right, b—bottom, t—top, c—centre, m—middle. We would like to thank the following for permission to reproduce photographs: Images © shutterstock; Pg2ml Rama, CC BY-SA 4.0 <https://creativecommons.org/licenses/by-sa/4.0>, via Wikimedia Commons, pg6-7tl Sasanan Trakansuebkul / Shutterstock.com, pg6c Purmak Marina / Shutterstock.com, pg9tr ChameleonsEye / Shutterstock.com, pg10tr Alexandros Michailidis / Shutterstock.com, pg10br Kosit / Shutterstock.com, pg11tr Sukhvinder Saggu / Shutterstock.com, pg10c Sasanan Trakansuebkul / Shutterstock.com, pg12 Holli / Shutterstock.com, pg14 ChameleonsEye / Shutterstock.com, pg15 Elena Chevalier / Shutterstock.com, pg18bl Claudine Van Massenhove / Shutterstock.com, pg19tl Rijksmuseum, CC0, via Wikimedia Commons, pg19tr David Steele / Shutterstock.com, pg20t Mitchell Library, State Library of New South Wales, pg20-21m State Library of New South Wales, Public domain, via Wikimedia Commons, pg21tl Norman HerfortNorman Herfort, Public domain, via Wikimedia Commons, pg22m 2WinG2 / Shutterstock.com, pg22br myphotobank.com.au / Shutterstock.com, pg23m Brisbane / Shutterstock.com, pg23bl doublelee / Shutterstock.com, pg24b Nicolas Economou / Shutterstock.com, pg25tl hikrcn / Shutterstock.com, pg25b hikrcn / Shutterstock.com, pg26 punghi / Shutterstock.com, pg27 Richard Milnes / Alamy Stock Photo, pg32tr Rama, CC BY-SA 4.0 <https://creativecommons.org/licenses/by-sa/4.0>, via Wikimedia Commons

NATIONAL LIBRARY OF AUSTRALIA
A catalogue record for this book is available from the National Library of Australia

CONTENTS

SPECIAL DAYS

In Australia, we celebrate or commemorate a number of special days throughout the year. Some are public holidays, which means that people can have the day off work or school. Some special days are marked with planned events and festivities.

Many special days in Australia commemorate something of historical importance. This gives Australians the opportunity to recognise how people and events have shaped our nation. Australia is a multicultural society with a federation of states and territories. Some special days are significant only to a particular state. Some are important to a specific culture, community or religious group.

Special days are a chance to reflect on the past, to appreciate the world we know and to look to the future together. On these days, we celebrate some of the things that make Australia what it is today.

HARMONY DAY

Since 1999, Australians have called 21 March, Harmony Day. It began as a positive day to celebrate, encourage and promote social solidarity and harmony among all Australians. Harmony Week aims to acknowledge and appreciate the diverse range of people, from different cultures and backgrounds, who call Australia home.

In 2019, on its 20th anniversary, Harmony Day celebrations were extended to a full week. This expansion has allowed local councils, schools and communities the time and space to engage deeper with the themes of cultural diversity and inclusion.

DAY: Harmony Day
(part of Harmony Week)
DATE: 21 March
WHERE: All states and territories
WHAT: Australian's come together to celebrate the positive benefits of multiculturalism. Harmony Day coincides with the United Nations International Day for the Elimination of Racial Discrimination.
Harmony Week is an important time to appreciate and learn about the contributions of different cultures in your community. Schools, workplaces and community organisations hold special events to celebrate cultural awareness, respect and inclusivity.

WEAR ORANGE TO SHOW EMPATHY, RESPECT AND UNDERSTANDING

On Harmony Day, we wear something orange to show our commitment to cultural harmony.

Orange clothing or orange accessories are a powerful tool that can start a conversation about racism, or simply show a member of a different culture that you care about and appreciate their cultural difference.

This simple act could have an enormous impact on a classmate, a friend or someone you don't even know yet!

The colour orange represents social communication, meaningful conversation, freedom of ideas and mutual respect.

MAKE IT COUNT

THE BIGGER PICTURE

Harmony Week is an important time to focus on actively thinking about cultural harmony. However, the elimination of racism must be active and ongoing, 365-days a year, and each of us has responsibility to act.

The best way to show empathy, respect and understanding is to learn about something that is special to another person.

1. **Share and listen to stories**
   Invite local elders to tell stories about their culture and traditions. Elders can be Indigenous Australians or respected members of a cultural group in your local community.

2. **Perform cultural songs or dances**
   Learning to perform a cultural song or dance is a profound way to share a cultural experience.

3. **Share cultural foods**
   Prepare a meal that is meaningful to your culture. Share it with others and talk about why this food is important to you.

4. **Wear your cultural dress**
   Do you have a traditional dress, or is a particular clothing style representative of your culture? Dress can be a fun way to express yourself!

4. **Talk about race and racism**
   Over to you! How do you feel about racism?

MULTICULTURAL FESTIVALS

Local councils and governments allocate public services and infrastructure to several cultural festivals throughout the year, including NAIDOC Week, Lunar New Year, Christmas, Greek Orthodox Easter, Ferragosto, Diwali, Vaisakhi and many others. These events are great examples of the high value that Australian's place on the celebration of multiculturalism and the preservation of cultural histories and traditions.

GREEK ORTHODOX EASTER

LIGHTS OF CHRISTMAS, ST MARY'S CATHEDRAL, SYDNEY

CHINESE LUNAR NEW YEAR

COMMUNITY EVENTS

During Harmony Week, thousands of cultural events and festivals are held all around Australia.

SIKH CULTURAL EVENT IN SYDNEY

Joining in with celebrations for cultural traditions that are different to your own can be a lot of fun and a great way to learn about a different culture.

Community events are a great way to learn about the diverse cultures in your community. During Harmony Week there may be a range of different festivals, celebrations, activities, performances and workshops.

HOLI AND HARMONY DAY CELEBRATIONS, CANBERRA

NATIVE LANGUAGE

Harmony Week remind us of the thousands of unique languages that are spoken all around the world.

The preservation of native languages is essential for maintaining cultural identity. Whilst language can be taught and learned in an educational setting, it is more meaningful to experience language through shared experiences.

Sharing or reading folktales, legends and myths are exciting ways to experience and appreciate traditional languages. Singing is another profound way to share how a language feels and can create a unique bonding experience.

AUSTRALIANS CELEBRATE THE WORLD'S OLDEST LIVING CULTURE AT BARANGAROO RESERVE, SYDNEY

COMFORT FOOD

Mealtimes are a traditional comfort in every culture. Food not only sustains our bodies, but it has a huge influence on our emotions and our connection to those we love. Food is connected to memory, place, culture and communication and has brought families and communities together for millennia.

Do you have a favourite dish that is special to your culture? Have you ever shared it with friends from different cultures? The next time you see a friend or schoolmate with interesting or unfamiliar foods, why not ask them about it? It is a great way to learn more about that person and gain a deeper understanding of the traditions and connections that are experienced through food.

ABORIGINAL AND TORRES STRAIT ISLANDER PEOPLES

Aboriginal and Torres Strait Islander peoples have been the custodians of Australia since the Dreaming. For tens of thousands of years, they have respectfully cared for its plants, animals and water supplies, and have nurtured the spiritual connections between all things.

Sadly, many areas of Australia's Indigenous culture became lost during colonisation, but there are now large groups of Indigenous and non-Indigenous people working together to better understand, and appropriately manage and preserve this essential part of Australia's history and heritage.

We pay particular attention to the celebration of culture during Harmony Week, but for many people, cultural preservation is a ever-present part of everyday life.

MIGRATION AND CULTURAL PRESERVATION

Migrant communities can find a strong sense of belonging when they come together to preserve the traditions and values of their unique cultures in their new homeland.

Sharing oral traditions by storytelling or singing, and reading or writing literary works can play an important role in the preservation of global histories and cultures.

Community groups organise activities and events as a way for people to connect with others who have common interests or shared histories. Some groups organise performances or cultural demonstrations to help recreate and share their heritage.

HISTORY OF HARMONY DAY IN AUSTRALIA

In 1998, the Australian Government conducted a research report into the state of racism in Australia. The findings were used to build an education campaign that was hoped might help to unify and harmonise Australia's various cultural groups.

On 21 March 1999, Harmony Day was introduced as a national day to celebrate Australia's diverse range of migrants who all contribute to the rich and varied development of our communities, businesses and overall wellbeing as a nation.

Harmony Week is now a celebration of a hope that multicultural communities can thrive, not in spite of one another, but rather, *because* of one another.

PARLIAMENT HOUSE, CANBERRA

Because Harmony Day coincides with the United Nations International Day for the Elimination of Racial Discrimination, it is essential that among the celebrations, we also acknowledge the enormous effect that racism has on individuals, communities and the prosperity of entire nations.

GET INVOLVED!

Every one of us has a part to play in the fight against racism. Even the smallest of actions can have an enormous impact.

HISTORY OF MULTICULTURALISM IN AUSTRALIA

Australia is one of the most multicultural countries in the world, with over 300 different ancestries contributing to our national identity. One in five people speak a language other than English at home and Australia's First Peoples have over 250 languages, with over 800 dialects!

Australia's First Peoples are the oldest continuous culture in the world. Today, over 49 percent of Australians were born overseas, or have a parent who was. Generations of Australians have ancestors who came from all over the world in search of a better life.

Since the First Fleet arrived in 1788, almost 10 million settlers have immigrated to Australia. First came the 160,000 British convicts, sentenced to transportation to relieve pressure on overcrowded prisons. Then came almost 200,000 free settlers, simply hoping for a better life.

When Australia struck gold in the 1850s, over 600,000 immigrants came within a decade, mostly from the UK, Europe and China. But not all the luck was in the goldfields and many found prosperity from supporting the prospectors. They opened shops and restaurants and began to form cultural hubs and communities. Afghan cameleers were vital to this development and to the exploration of the Australian outback.

PEARL DIVERS, 1939

Between 1863 and 1901, over 62,000 South Sea Islanders were transported as forced labour for Queensland's sugar plantations.

In 1901, Australia introduced its White Australia policy which halted non-European immigration. However, the colonists had discovered Australia's 20,000-year-old pearling industry and needed the knowledge and labour of Aboriginal and Torres Strait Islander peoples as well as the talented divers from Asia.

Between the 1880s and 1942, about 6,000 Japanese divers were granted exemption from the White Australia policy. These divers helped secure Broome as the pearling capital of the world.

In 1945, the Australian Government introduced the Assisted Passage Migration Scheme.

Introduced in Britain and the Republic of Ireland the scheme provided passage to Australia for just ten British pounds. In a push to build the nation, the Australian Government needed to attract immigrants who could assimilate quickly. These 'ten-pound Poms' spoke the same language and, for the most part, shared similar beliefs and cultural values.

THE MV GEORGIC MIGRANT SHIP ARRIVES IN AUSTRALIA, FEBRUARY 1949

Between 1949 and 1973, the set of policies that made up the White Australia policy were gradually dismantled, although many racist and discriminatory aspects have remained. There are complex issues behind these policies which remain difficult for governments to reconcile.

MODERN MIGRANTS

Australia is a well-respected education hub with world-class universities and a range of skilled employment opportunities. The safe and welcoming environment, cultural diversity and natural beauty of Australia continue to attract immigrants in their thousands.

Darwin

Western Australia

Perth

TOP FIVE MULTICULTURAL HUBS BY STATE

1. **New South Wales** – Sydney
2. **Victoria** – Melbourne
3. **Queensland** – Brisbane
4. **Western Australia** – Perth
5. **South Australia** – Adelaide

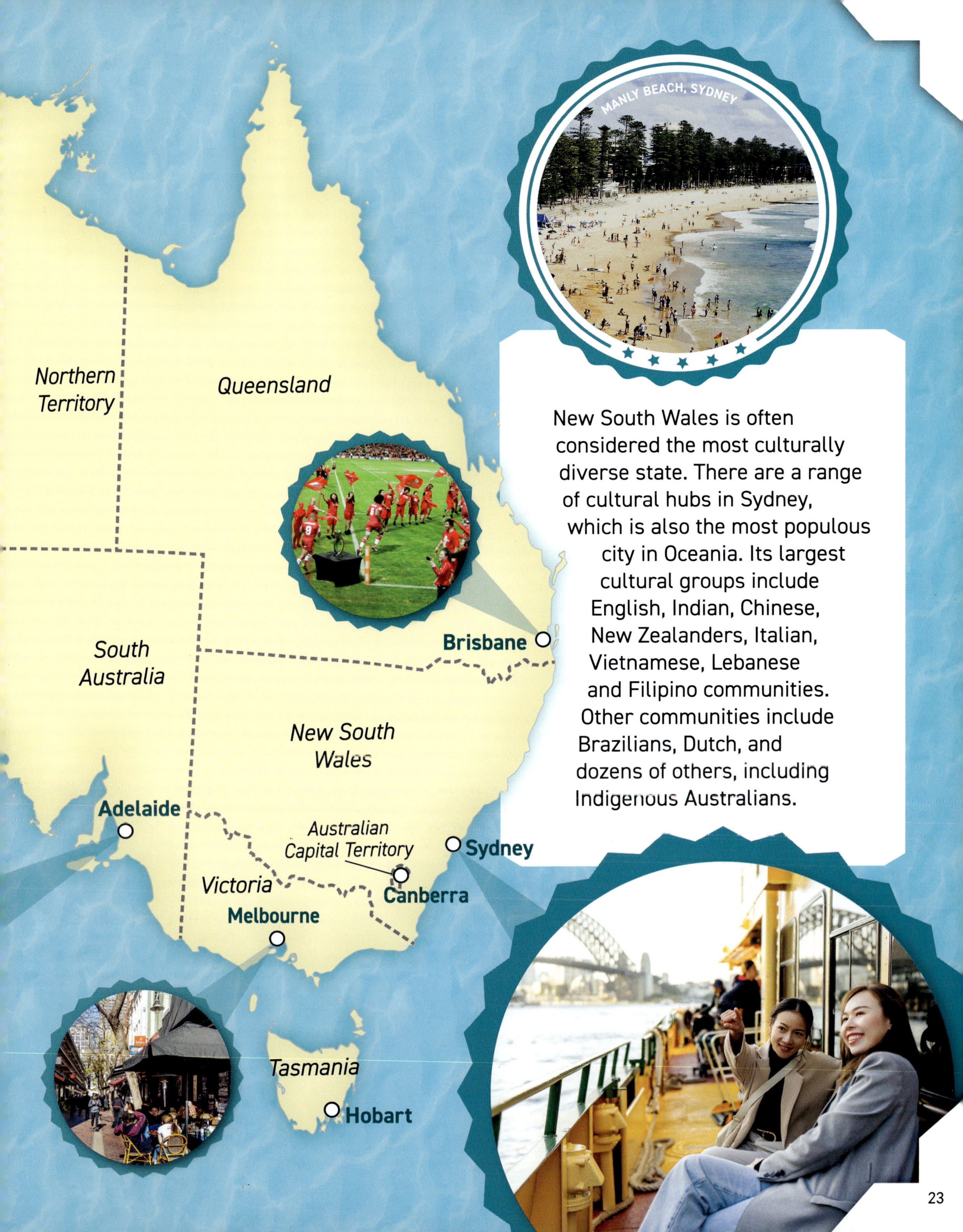

New South Wales is often considered the most culturally diverse state. There are a range of cultural hubs in Sydney, which is also the most populous city in Oceania. Its largest cultural groups include English, Indian, Chinese, New Zealanders, Italian, Vietnamese, Lebanese and Filipino communities. Other communities include Brazilians, Dutch, and dozens of others, including Indigenous Australians.

FORCED MIGRATION

Migration has shaped communities around the world for millennia. People move for work, study, to be closer to family, or simply for a better life. However, not all migrants choose to move. Every year, millions of people are forced to flee their homes because it is no longer safe to stay there. This can be due to war, persecution, environmental disaster or a lack of human rights.

SYRIAN REFUGEES ARRIVE IN GREECE

ASYLUM SEEKERS

People who need to leave their homeland because of an unsafe situation can ask another country to protect them. This is called 'seeking asylum'. If granted, asylum allows people to live safely in a new country.

Sometimes people are allowed to live in the community while the government makes a decision, sometimes they are made to live in big camps, and sometimes they are placed in detention.

Most asylum seekers and refugees have lived through terrifying situations. They may have been hurt or injured. They may have lost loved ones and have limited or no support from friends or family.

DADAAB REFUGEE CAMP, SOMALIA

REFUGEES

People who fear for their lives and their family's lives must make extraordinary decisions. Illegal people smugglers make enormous sums of money by offering passage to desperate people with nothing to lose.

Many refugees flee with little or no possessions and no identification documents. In times of crisis, when many people may flee at the same time, there is often no access to migration services for travel visas or passports. This can make travel by ordinary means impossible since airlines risk heavy fines for carrying passengers without valid passports and visas.

STORYTELLING TO THE MASSES

Anh Do is a Vietnamese-born Australian artist, comedian, actor and author, but most importantly, he is *The Happiest Refugee*. When Anh Do was three years old, his family fled the war in Vietnam on a small, wooden fishing boat that leaked. They were attacked by pirates twice before being saved by a German cargo ship, and spent time in a Malaysian refugee camp before finally arriving in Australia.

Anh Do is now a famous and well-respected Australian. He is able to use his position as a successful media personality to be able to tell the stories of his home country to audiences all around the world! He is both a proud Australian and a tireless advocate for the preservation of Vietnamese culture and tradition, which are central forces in his identity and his work.

A CHALLENGING TIME

New migrants can face a range of challenges in their new country. Language barriers can make it harder to make new friends and can create difficulties at school. It is also normal for new migrants to feel a huge sense of loss for the people and places they left behind. They may also feel insecure or anxious if they left an unsafe place.

If new migrants experience discrimination, prejudice or bullying, this can have a huge impact on their sense of belonging and self-esteem.

A sense of belonging is the feeling of being accepted, valued, and connected to a group, community, or environment. It means feeling secure and appreciated for who you are.

SUPPORTING NEW MIGRANTS

Every new migrant has a right to feel safe and supported. If you know of a new migrant in your local community, it's important to help them feel welcome.

1. **Be inclusive and welcoming**
   Invite them to join group activities and conversations. Offer to show them around or introduce them to people you know.

2. **Learn about their culture**
   Show interest in their culture and language, and ask about their home country and experiences.

3. **Stand up against bullying**
   Be an ally and advocate for inclusivity, respect and kindness.

SAY WHAT?

Even the best student of textbook English will rarely be prepared for the way Australians actually talk! Different dialects, slang language and colloquialisms can be very confusing even for the most confident new English speakers.

INTO THE FUTURE

Every country across the globe has experienced the movement of people, as the world becomes increasingly accessible to those with wealth and increasingly volatile for those without.

Multiculturalism is a valuable product of the movement of people and the elimination of racism is absolutely essential to the future of the world.

GLOSSARY

advocate argue for the cause of another
colloquialism informal word or phrase
belonging human emotional need to be an accepted member of a group
culture ideas, customs, and behaviours of a people or society
belonging human emotional need to be an accepted member of a group
detention being officially forced to stay in a place
discrimination unfair treatment of people based on difference
diverse different types of people
heritage culture that is handed down through generations
identity feeling that you are a particular type of person
immigrant person who comes to live permanently in a foreign country
persecution ill-treatment, especially on the basis of ethnicity
preservation action of preserving something
racism belief that humans may be divided into separate and exclusive biological entities
refugee person who has been forced to leave their country in order to escape war, persecution, or natural disaster
solidarity unity or agreement of feeling or action, especially among individuals with a common interest

INDEX